Hoodoo Book of Spells for Beginners

Easy and effective Rootwork, Conjuring, and

Protection Spells for Healing and Prosperity

Layla Moon

Hoodoo Book of Spells for Beginners

Hoodoo Book of Spells for Beginners

Table of Contents

Your FREE Gifts

To help you along your spiritual journey, I've created 4 FREE bonus eBooks.

You can get instant access by signing up to my email newsletter below.

On top of the 4 free books, you will also receive weekly tips along with free book giveaways, discounts, and so much more.

All of these bonuses are 100% free with no strings attached. You don't need to provide any personal information except your email address.

To get your bonus, go to:

https://dreamlifepress.com/four-free-gifts

Or scan the QR code below

Spirit Guides for Beginners: How to Hear the Universe's Call and Communicate with Your Spirit Guide and Guardian Angels

Guided by Moon herself, inspired by her own experiences and knowledge that has been passed down by hundreds of generations for thousands of years, you'll discover everything you need to know to;

- Understanding what the call of the universe is
- How to hear and comprehend it
- Knowing who and what your spirit guides and guardian angels are
- Learning how to connect, start a conversation, and listen to your guides
- How to manifest your dreams with the help of the cosmic source
- Learning how to start living the life you want to live
- And so much more…

Law of Attraction: Manifest Your Desire

Learn how to tap into the infinite power of the universe and manifest everything you want in life.

Includes:

- Law of Attraction: Manifest Your Desire ebook
- Law of Attraction Workbook
- Cheat sheets and checklists so make sure you're on the right path

Book of Shadows

A printable PDF to support you in your spiritual transformation.

Within the pages, you will find:

- Potion and tinctures tracking sheet
- Essential oils log pages
- Herbs log pages
- Magical rituals and spiritual body goals checklist
- Tarot reading spread sheets
- Weekly moon and planetary cycle tracker
- And so much more

Get all the resources for FREE by visiting the link below

https://dreamlifepress.com/four-free-gifts

Introduction

It was during the hardest times that I discovered Hoodoo, and the power that this sorcery holds.

I've dabbled with various spiritual practices throughout my life, but few of them have stuck with me in the way Hoodoo has. Originating within the African American populations, mainly in the southern United States, Hoodoo magic is a relatively new form of magic on the grand scale of time, but its impact has changed the lives of endless people across the world indefinitely.

While not as popular today as it once was, Hoodoo magic still plays a big part in the lives of those who practice it - practitioners known as rootworkers or root doctors, but don't let this mislead you. Hoodoo is so much more than the chemistry and alchemy of roots, herbs, and spices, as you'll discover throughout this book.

My Personal Experience Awakened

I've personally been familiar with Hoodoo from a young age. While my parents were Jehovah's Witnesses, it was always Hoodoo magic that held a special place in my heart. Magic that interested me in a way I couldn't quite describe.

My grandmother was someone who swore by it. I remember sitting and watching her create potions in her home, going out and collecting ingredients wherever she could, and playing with some of the more elaborately designed bottles and potion vials she had collected over the years.

But still, I struggled to grasp Hoodoo myself. Although I was introduced all those years ago, I had yet to give myself to the practice and open myself up. In hindsight, I now understand it was simply that the time wasn't right. In fact, that time didn't come until around a decade ago when I was sitting in my apartment during some of my darker days. My emotions stewed inside me despite all my tears having already flowed.

I had found myself in a bad relationship. An explosively violent one. I now see my ex-partner living with his own demons, and while I'm still sure we loved each other in our own way, we weren't meant to be. Regardless, it was during one of the more intense fights I truly started to realize this for perhaps the first time. He had left our apartment and went to stay with a friend. I was left alone in my own space, hunched over at the kitchen table in the darkness, the only light coming from the streetlight on the other side of the street.

I was lost, confused, and entirely unsure of what my future held. It was at this moment, literally sitting with my head in my hands, that the shimmers of Hoodoo began to draw my attention gently. At first, I was taken a little by surprise, but this was soon replaced by feelings of intrigue and curiosity. All the little pieces of information I had discovered over the years slowly started to piece themselves together inside my mind in a way they had not done before. The curiosity seemed to consume me.

I pulled out a book my grandmother had passed down

to me many years before from the bookcase and flicked through the pages for an hour or so, not really sure what I was looking for. Eventually, about midway through, I came across a recipe for a potion of happiness. I laughed to myself. Could it really be that simple?

I thought back to my grandmother all those years ago. I had so much love and respect for that lady in my life, so hey, if she was adamant it worked, then maybe I should be too. It took a while and a strange walk outside in the middle of the night to the Bronx park, but I managed to collect all the ingredients.

I searched the apartment for bits and pieces I could use. The book was old, torn at the spine with several missing pages, but most were present. It was a book of protection spells and described roots, herbs, spices,

A little under an hour later, the potion was set, and I recited the spell written among the pages. I also spent a few minutes writing down any intentions I had onto small scraps of paper, folding them up and tying them to the potion vial, and sat with the setup for half an hour or so and meditating on my intentions.

At first, I thought I wanted freedom from my suffering, and there's no doubt I did. My sadness was almost overwhelming, and I just wanted it to end. This was my main intention, but this quickly faded to the back of my mind, and without warning, made way for something a little more profound.

I felt peaceful. I felt calm, but I also felt determined. There was a moment, a lasting moment in the stillness, that seemed to stretch on and on where I felt determined. I felt motivated. I felt driven. I knew I was in a rut, but I would feel a burning drive within me that knew that if I put my mind to it, I would be able to move forward.

At the time, I thought it was simply a moment of realization. An epiphany, and perhaps to some degree it was. However, I know now, coupled with my more recent experiences over the years, that this was some kind of magic. Ever since, time and time again, I've been able to tap into this source of power that's not just within me but a kind of magic that's within us all.

What is Hoodoo Magic?

At its core, by dictionary definition, Hoodoo is an art form used to conjure, manifest, and exchange physical and spiritual powers. A magic used to generate and attract wealth, good health, increased fortunes, and to improve relationships. A magic used to help you define your intentions and to give you a sense of direction that enables you to overcome and conquer any challenges or obstacles you may face at any point in your life.

It's a set of spiritual practices, traditions, and beliefs with origins rooted in the Black African communities that North America and Europeans wrongfully enslaved over the last 300 years. A way for human beings to allow supernatural forces into their lives in an attempt to improve them.

The word 'Hoodoo' first appeared in written documents around 1870, but the true origins are unknown. As you may have guessed from the spelling, the word is believed to have originated from the word 'Voodoo,' although the two practices are quite different, as will be explained later in this chapter.

As painful as it is to conceptualize, over 12 million people were enslaved and transported from the African continent to North America (what is now the United States) between the 16th and 19th Centuries, a truly traumatic experience, the effects and consequences of which still ripple out around the world through people like us to this day.

It was within these enslaved, African, becoming African-American communities, the art of Hoodoo found its feet, rooting itself in the culture to eventually blossom into what it is today.

However, a form of Hoodoo was already practiced in Africa, but here it was regarded as a religion, but soon became regarded as a way of magic. Allow me to bring some perspective to this.

If you lived in 18th Century American as a Black slave, you did not share the same medical care as those living in the European-American communities. Black communities, therefore, needed to create their own support and healthcare systems and their own ways of looking after themselves, both for the enslaved and free. This includes psychological care, emotional and spiritual support, and so on.

Black communities had no choice but to rely on the knowledge and spirit of the people around them, those who were also suffering. With nowhere to go and no one to turn to, they had only the love, support, and knowledge of each other. It was within this practice of care, communication, and the coming togetherness that allowed those in suffering to process their trauma and find some kind of healing from the tragic situations they found themselves in.

Since enslaved people were taken from all over the African continent, they came from various cultures, societies, and ethnic backgrounds. With such diversity coming together in one place, Hoodoo was a way of bringing these people together in a union of respect and compassion. Hoodoo is, therefore, almost a cocktail of magic, love, respect, and community from all these various places that would otherwise have not come together. I believe that that, in a beautiful way, is a kind of magic in itself.

This means modern Hoodoo is a mixture of religion and magical practices that have all come together under severely intense circumstances, making it one of the most powerful forces there is.

There's no doubt the significant influences of Hoodoo come from the Central African regions. Evidence suggests around 40% of all enslaved Africans came from these central regions, specifically the Bantu-Kongo areas. This is evident within Hoodoo practices since there are clear links to the Kongo cosmogram and Kongolese beliefs and practices.

The other significant influence comes from the

Western African region, introducing various components, such as the magical mojo bag. Many of the ships traveling to and from North America landed on the West African coast, from where the slave trade was managed and organized. It should come as no surprise that there were sadly many people enslaved from this area. There is also clear evidence of magical influence from West African Muslim communities, whose members resided in these areas during slave trading periods.

Nowadays, Hoodoo is practiced within the more subtle veins of society. Its practitioners are often called 'root workers' or 'root doctors' since they emphasize working with herbs, roots, and plants. Although it's most often referred to as 'root working,' in general, it's important to remember that this is just one aspect of Hoodoo practice.

Interestingly, what sets Hoodoo apart from other forms of Western or European magic, and what makes it appealing to many, is that there's no need to practice any kind of summoning, nor do you need to negotiate or form relationships with other spirits, forms, or entities. While the 19th Century brought about a lot of Christian influence in the practice, Hoodoo practitioners do believe in a God of sorts, but there's not a significant emphasis on the God themselves.

The Hoodoo God is a genderless entity, but they are neither good nor evil, despite very strong ideas on what good and evil are within Hoodoo practices. God is the supreme being responsible for the creation of the world, but this God is not concerned with the goings-on of humankind. There are lesser entities and spirits that are involved in these activities.

The Boo Hag is one such spirit. An umbrella term, a Boo Hag is a spirit that exists to torment and scare living people. They have magical, spiritual powers that can kill or cure people of diseases, predict the future, or help people find things.

When you consider where Hoodoo magic came from, you should see why this makes sense. For example, populations of African Americans in Indiana refused to enter a certain location because it was 'haunted by the spirits of the Black people who were beaten to death.' This is the work of the Boo Hag.

But not all spirits are evil or come from a place of pain, misfortune, and torment. There are spirits that protect from pain and suffering, spirits that bring peace and calm to intense situations or settle intense feelings, and spirits that reside within the elements, such as the MIA, the West African water spirit.

However, while I could write an entire book on the history and the spiritual world of Hoodoo, the most important thing to remember about the history is the fact that it was born out of suffering and is a practice deeply rooted in the hearts and the lives of your ancestors.

This is where the magic gets its power.

The Links Between Voodoo and Hoodoo

Hoodoo magic is not Voodoo magic, and there are some core similarities and differences you may want to help better your understanding of what this practice is actually all about.

This is the first distinction you need to make. There are similarities, but the two are not the same, but they are certainly related. In mainstream culture, Hoodoo is very much used to describe any form of native American or African culture magic. Voodoo is a religion, also known as a magical tradition. Both have elements of African and European influence.

However, Hoodoo has loose ties with Catholic Christianity, whereas Voodoo has ties with Protestant Christianity. Don't mistake that practitioners have to be Christian following in any sense.

Voodoo magic is very much its own religious practice, one that stems from countries like Haiti, with some ties to West African populations. Within Voodoo, you must walk the path that gets you ordained in the religion, and there must be leaders present to oversee the magic performed. There are also numerous deities, gods, entities, and spirits that must be worshiped and respected for the practices to be followed correctly.

None of these requirements are necessary, nor exist, within Hoodoo practices. Practitioners don't need to believe or follow any gods, and you're free to worship any other Gods or deities you may respect or believe in. There's no ruling hierarchy to follow, such as having overseers, priests, or other ordained individuals who would theoretically be 'higher up' than you.

Hoodoo has no strict structure that needs to be followed like in other religions. Hoodoo is a practice that you find and connect with within yourself for your own benefit. You're not trying to serve some greater purpose or worship an entity. That's why Hoodoo can be best described as personal magic.

In the modern world, the terms Hoodoo and Voodoo are very much used interchangeably, even though this is wrong. It's simply a misconception by those who don't know any better. In reality, modern Hoodoo, especially 'non-African' Hoodoo, seems to borrow some aspects of Voodoo magic but is more seen by those who practice it as a more Christianized variation of the well-established and more dominantly practiced Voodoo that is practiced in countries like Haiti.

Remember, despite the popular opinion that the mainstream public seems to hold on Voodoo being used for evil purposes, this is just not the case. Hoodoo seems to fall under this category for a lot of people for the same reasons, but the opposite is right. Both Voodoo and Hoodoo can be used for good, for healing, and for prosperity, but there can be more malicious practices, should that be what the user intends to use the magic for, as there can be for any substance of practice in this world.

To cut a long story short, Hoodoo is not Voodoo. There are certainly similarities, but they are not the same. There are many varieties of each, and for this book, we're going to be focusing mainly on Black

Hoodoo, or the Hoodoo created by the African American communities. Interestingly, this is a magic that stems from African Voodoo, but with European influence, since it was created when Europeans took slaves to America, and the two cultures intertwined, hence the Christian influences.

As you'll see later on, this is why many of Hoodoo spells use recitals from the psalms and bible passages, and there are many ties to Christian passages.

There is also a stem of Hoodoo known as 'White Hoodoo,' but this is the term given to practitioners who don't have African origins. These are still non-white people, but they weren't enslaved by other Africans, nor come from African descent.

Due to the history of Hoodoo, it's a magic only Black people can practice.

CHAPTER ONE

Hoodoo in the Modern World

"In hoodooism, anything that you do is the plan of God, understand? God has something to do with everything that you do whether it's good or bad, he's got something to do with it... You'll get what's coming to you." - Translated practitioner

In today's modern world, there are issues and difficulties I've experienced, and there's no doubt these problems have affected you in some way at some point in your life. Aspects of your life like money, relationships, landlords, careers, health, and everything else that affects you, both big and small.

One thing you can be sure of in life is that it's going to throw curveballs and challenges your way. You need to figure out how to deal with these situations for the sake of your own health, wellbeing, and inner peace.

Hoodoo is a methodology, a process, and an art form that can help you to find the answers you're looking for. It's a spiritual practice to help you reconnect with yourself at your core, not just with who you are as an individual, but also with your history. Your ancestry. Your past.

Hoodoo acts as a light to illuminate your way during the darker times. It holds back and protects you from shadows that may be lurking on the horizon, just out of sight.

My experience with Hoodoo has been one of progression and salvation, the results of which have encouraged me to write about them in the hopes that you can feel inspired enough to open your heart and your mind to the wonders of Hoodoo.

It's not an easy task. Hoodoo's history is long and stems from a dark place. A place of pain and suffering, but that's one part of life that will never change. Instead, it's time to make peace with this discomfort by embracing it and overcoming it. It may sound a little scary, but this book exists to guide you to a place where this is possible.

You've come so far already, and by holding this book in your hands right now, it's a sign you're ready to take the next step. I know, deep down in my very essence, that you're seeking the same thing that I once did, and now you're on the cusp of discovery.

You seek answers. You crave a path to walk. You're determined to discover clarity. There's a spark inside you, burning for you to reconnect with yourself, your instinct, and your inner and spiritual being. It's time to learn how to trust yourself and your inner knowledge, unlocking your full potential in any situation. It's time to manifest your desires, your wants, and to start living the life you want.

To some, this may seem like an impossible idea, but it isn't.

Never before has an intentional art such as Hoodoo been more important or so potentially valuable in the lives of so many people. Becoming familiar with such an art can unlock so many doors within your life while helping you move past the potential obstacles that hold you back.

Throughout the following chapters, we're going to explore the ins and outs of Hoodoo ideas, sharing the knowledge that has been passed down for generations.

I'm going to dive into the history of Hoodoo, where it came from, and what stories make up this practice's origins. We'll explore the rules and guidelines and how you can start to master the process and use it in your day-to-day life.

This book will serve as a beginner's guide. An introduction. A nudge in the right direction provides enough information to get you started and stand firmly on your own two feet.

This isn't about some long-lost magic or practice that creates wondrous effects as you see in movies. This is about intention.

This is about connecting your mind with your spirit and your soul. It's about healing and processing traumas and protecting yourself from any dangers you may encounter in the future. It's about finding peace during the hardest times so you can shine brightly once again.

If, for the last few years, and perhaps many years of your life, you have been stricken with darkness and troubles, by turning these pages, you allow yourself the opportunity to light a candle to find your way.

And with that, set the spark that sets this journey off in the best possible way. The candle is lit.

Turn the page and go forth.

How to Use Hoodoo in the Modern World

Hoodoo was born out of a need. It stemmed from the pain and suffering of Black people. Therefore, it's a magic that only Black people can practice. In the past, it would have been used for all kinds of purposes, including:

- Promoting happiness within families and communities

- Increasing fortunes and chances of favorable situations

- Reducing feelings of pain and suffering

- Healing traumas and both physical and emotional hurt

- Nurturing protection again future dangers

- Exacting revenge on those who cause pain

These are clearly situations that haunt many of us today, and you've perhaps experienced them already. Times are turbulent, and perhaps to an extent they always will be, which is why Hoodoo will remain relevant.

If you want to practice Hoodoo and you want to experience this magic in your life, you need to be able to connect to its history and its origins on a deeper level and relate this pain, suffering, and togetherness to your own. Yes, it can be painful, and it hurts. Yes, it can be traumatic, and there are places, certainly in your own past, that you may not want to go to, but you need to open your mind to the call of your ancestors to channel their energy.

We'll take things step by step, but remind yourself that there is no need to be scared. Or afraid. This is a path many have walked, and many will walk after you. Open your soul, and let's walk together.

And it's on that note that you should now be ready to take your first steps into the world of Hoodoo. It's time to reconnect with this magical practice and see the benefits for yourself.

Take a deep breath as you reconnect with this historical power, turn to your new chapter, and let's begin.

CHAPTER TWO

Getting Started with Rootwork/Hoodoo

"The psychic witch lives in a state of enchantment, seeing all things as magickal and understanding that the universe is composed of endless possibilities and potential. The psychic witch sees a door where others see a wall."— Mat Auryn

When I first started to connect with my magical core, I felt a mix of emotions. I was excited and curious about what was going to happen, but I would be lying if I didn't say I was a little scared. After all, what was going to happen? What happened if I accidentally connected with some profound dark energy or spirit, some entity of trauma and suffering that I couldn't escape?

These fears certainly crossed my mind, but I knew that my intention was clear and pure deep down in my heart. I wanted to find peace, and I wanted to discover a light that could lead me through my own darkness. Since my own personal journey began during some of the darker times of my life, I wanted to push through my insecurities to find out more.

But it's important to remember you don't need to walk alone. There are many people on the same path as you, people starting out and those who will start out, and I, too, was once in your position. There is also the entirety of your ancestors behind you, the people from whom you came from; many of whom would have been involved with their own Hoodoo practices and may have even been there at its origin.

When getting started with Hoodoo practices, you first need to open your mind to this realization. You need to do the same with your soul and your heart. Open yourself to the magical guidance that lies before you.

If you want to be elevated through the magic, you need to let it in, and while this notion may seem easy, it's a tricky thing to do and not something that will happen overnight.

Unfortunately, opening your mind is not something that can be strictly taught but is instead a process of crossing the obstacles in your way as you discover them. Opportunities will come and go, such as if you're having a particularly stressful time. It's when you become mindful that this stressful or painful time is, in fact, an opportunity to connect to Hoodoo magic that you'll start to see what it's capable of. It starts with mindfulness.

For example, if you find your relationship is on the rocks and you're experiencing difficulties, it's easy to find yourself back in the conditioned patterns of arguing or trying to score points. Perhaps you're the kind of person who hides away and pushes all those negative feelings down and tries to ignore them as best you can until you feel like exploding.

It's during challenging times like this where you'll need to remind yourself about the power of Hoodoo magic and what it can do for you. It all starts with intention.

No matter what you're doing, what aspect of your life you're working with, or what spells you're practicing, the power of your actions will rely on the intentions behind them. For now, focus on how Hoodoo magic can help you.

There's perhaps a reason you picked up this book in the first place and a reason why you wanted to try Hoodoo magic. Let this guide you into opening yourself up to what's possible.

When you're getting started with your own connection to Hoodoo, this openness is what you will need to focus on most. Throughout the following pages of this book, from the next chapter onwards, we're going to be exploring the ins and outs of certain conjuring, protection, and healing spells, as well as some of the substances and natural products that have Hoodoo effects.

Preparing for Your Journey

We've covered the mindset aspects of readying yourself for your journey into Hoodoo, but now let's get a little more practical. While Hoodoo is a practice about connecting to the supernatural, there are some physical actions you need to take, such as collecting and working with objects and materials.

Most of these are simple, natural products that African-Americans would have had access to back in the 16th Century, such as plants, candles, leaves, bits of metal, and other magical trinkets like divination cards or totems.

Personal concerns are also commonly used in spells, especially when the spells or potions are directed at someone specific. Such concerns include things like locks of hair, nail clippings, blood, pieces of bone, or other forms of bodily fluids. Of course, you're not expecting to acquire a piece of bone from someone. This kind of spell would have been used to help someone who died while suffering to have a peaceful transition out of the physical realm into the spiritual realm.

Nevertheless, you want to start focusing on building up your collection of natural products and concerns from people you want to cast spells on, as well as containers. Some common products you'll want to collect include;

- Glass vials and bottles for storing potions

- Purses and fabric pouches for storing powders and grounded materials

- Candles of any color and design

- Matches or a lighter to light candles or burn spell components

- A pen and paper (or a special Hoodoo notebook) for writing down spells and intentions

- An assortment of plant roots and natural herbs

- Stones, minerals, and crystals

- Divination materials like incense, pinnacles, or tarot cards

- Oils, wax, amulets, charms, clothing, incense, and pendants

- The hair, bodily fluids, or concerns from yourself or another person

On this note, I do highly recommend getting yourself a special notebook for recording all your Hoodoo practices. Not only can you write down the spells and intentions you want to focus on, but also notes on your experience. You can write down how you feel and how spells worked for you, or perhaps what you would do differently next time.

Having this journey written down is invaluable because it will help you become a better and better practitioner, thus improving your skills, conjuring, and casting abilities, and will ultimately enhance your Hoodoo experiences tenfold.

When you start learning the spells themselves and begin having a preference for the kind of spells and potions you want to work with, you can start becoming a little more familiar with the ingredients you want, but it's always a good idea to keep an eye open for potential materials you could use.

And when you have your materials in place, you're ready to begin.

CHAPTER THREE

Introducing the Art of Conjuring

"If people don't face the danger that's seeking them, evil will find them first."

I experimented for well over a year with different spells and ways of using Hoodoo magic, trying to figure out what worked for me and what didn't, and no matter what I tried, I always ended up back in the same place with the same kind of spells. These were conjuring spells, or manifestation spells, as they are sometimes referred to.

There are different beliefs as to what these kinds of spells can do and their limits, but at their core, the power and intention of these spells remain the same and, therefore, can be used in many different ways. To conjure or to manifest is to put something that doesn't exist into your physical world through the power of intentions, thoughts, willingness, and belief.

Now, this, of course, doesn't mean that you can simply close your eyes and manifest a million dollars to appear in front of you in a shiny black briefcase. The physical world is bound by limitations that prevent this from happening and being possible, but that doesn't mean you can't manifest a million dollars into your life in other ways. This kind of conjuring would be more along the lines of conjuring financial security and comfort.

To conjure something in your life is to put yourself in a mindset where you can make it happen. You are literally going through the process of conjuring what you want and bringing it into your life. Throughout your life, you may think about conjuring:

- The relationships you want

- The career you want

- Financial security

- The house or car you want

- A promotion you want

- The completion of a dream you've always had, such as writing a book or running a marathon

The list of possibilities is endless, and you're only limited by your imagination. In my own life, I manifested the focus and creativity to write this book. I managed to protect and help myself heal from the trauma of my past relationships. I've promoted good fortune when going for job interviews, approaching new clients, and meeting new people.

When I've felt stressed, anxious, or overwhelmed, I've used Hoodoo to bring myself back to a grounded state of mind and found new and creative ways to overcome the obstacles and difficult situations I've found myself in. This was all achieved through the power of Hoodoo conjuration spells.

Conjuration literally means to cast a magic spell or incantation. In Hoodoo, this is to create a connection to the spiritual realm, allowing supernatural forces to enter your life and create an effect that will positively benefit you. This could be manifesting good luck, shielding yourself from harm, and so on.

It really doesn't matter what you want in your life, Hoodoo is a way of helping you get from A to B and turning your intentions into your reality, all thanks to the help of supernatural forces, spirits, and entities. To cast a spell is to connect with these beings, communicating and conjuring their presence into life, depending on what you're trying to achieve.

So, how does this work, and how do you cast such conjuring spells? Let's look at a detailed example of how the Hoodoo conjuration process works and then some of the ways you can introduce these spells into your own life.

Imagine you wake up one day, and you're in a fantastic mood.

You're well-rested and energized, and you're looking forward to a great day. Because you're in such a good mood, you start asking yourself what you want to achieve for the day. Because you want to achieve these goals, you take time to cast a spell of good fortune, thus increasing your luck for whatever situations you find yourself in.

Through the act of casting the spell, you've set a message out to the supernatural forces of the universe to come to you to assist you in your endeavors. As the day goes on, you'll find yourself in increasingly more favorable situations.

Perhaps you'll receive an email you've been waiting for. Maybe your boss will have a meeting you've been waiting for about a promotion, or a client will get back to you about your proposal. These are the supernatural forces at work, slightly pulling on the strings behind the scenes to ensure everything aligns when it needs to, mostly in the tiniest ways that we could never comprehend.

As you set out into your day, you're thinking about these goals, and your brain is focused on making them happen. Anything that comes your way, whether things, people, or experiences, that will help you take a step towards the fulfillment of these goals, you'll treat them with gratitude and compassion.

This is all thanks to the guidance of supernatural forces ensuring you're in the right place at the right time, and their impact outside your immediate reality.

Of course, conjuration magic doesn't have to be used in such a subtle way or for such a 'positive' reason. If you were in a friendship, but your friend did something really hurtful to you, such as sleeping with your partner, spreading rumors about you, or ruining your reputation, you could conjure supernatural forces to address this issue.

You can use the magic to conjure a protective shield around yourself, heal a wound (physical or emotional) that has been created from the situation, or even redirecting the negative energy back at the person who sent it to you in the first place, giving them a taste of what they're doing, hopefully teaching them the lesson not to do it again.

The act of conjuration is literally to conjure or summon spirits to assist you in your life. How you summon the spirit will determine the spirit that helps and for what purpose it's going to serve you. As you'll see later on in the book, this usually involves some kind of ritual and magical practice, as well as ingredients and spell components, as we spoke about before.

From influencing people to fall in love with you, opening up new opportunities, protecting yourself, becoming more creative, or healing pains, Hoodoo magic provides a solution.

And with that, you should know everything you need to know when it comes to solidly understanding what Hoodoo and rootwork are all about. Now it's time to take a proper first step into this new world.

CHAPTER FOUR

Rootwork Spells for Conjuring and Manifestation

"One you'll soon learn is that while preparations for a spell can be complicated, the spells themselves will be quite easy to perform. "

For now, that's enough theorizing. It's time to get into the practical part of this book. With your mind open and your intentions to learn the techniques and conjure fresh in your mind, it's time to connect to Hoodoo power and channel it into your day-to-day life.

Bear in mind that some of the spells and their ingredients may sound a little complicated, or it feels like there's a lot of little bits and pieces you'll need to collect. It can take some time to build up your collection of magical items but note that many components can be used interchangeably among spells. Once you have access to a component, chances are you'll be using it for many years to come.

Now, allow me to show you the way.

Incense: The Most Common Way to Conjure

Spells can be difficult to put together, especially when you need to collect all the components, but there is an obvious way you can cast a small conjuring spell at any time, and that's by burning incense.

There are countless forms of incense out there, and you can almost perform the spell as a kind of mediation. All you need is an incense holder, preferably with an ash catcher, and whatever kind of incense you want to burn.

Simply place your incense in the holder, light it, and sit with it for a few minutes. The longer you sit and essentially meditate with the burning incense, the more powerful the spell, and therefore your intention, will be. Just sit with it, smell the aromas, and mindfully try to connect with that Hoodoo power source within you and within the universe.

As you sit, breathing deeply, stay as present as possible, and try to nudge your mind in the direction of your intentions. Take a moment to think about what you want and some of the ways you could go about getting it. Don't try to be solid with your reason, but rather let your instinct flow and see what comes to mind. Be fluid, like water. See what comes up and release your conditioned ways of thinking.

For example, you might try to think of some ways to be happier and more motivated at work, but as you think about it, you start to realize you're actually not in a job you want to be in, and instead you want to pursue a more fulfilling career. This kind of realization is the Hoodoo magic at work, so allow it to be, rather than dismissing it as hopeful thinking.

With that, here are some of the types of incense you may want to look into for conjuring and helping to increase and improve your focus and intention.

- Palo Santo is great if you're looking to heal something in your life. It's said to increase your energy vibrations and calm your body.

- Frankincense is ideal if you're looking to relieve stress and gain more awareness. If you're struggling and feel lost, this is the incense to help bring clarity.

- If you're seeking success and prosperity, you can burn Star Anise or Cinnamon incense to help bring you into a state of mind where you're making the best decisions in this area.

- Lavender is the incense of balance. If you need calm, clarity, and peace for setting intentions, discovering them, or reconnecting with yourself or the Hoodoo source, this is an excellent incense for clearing the mind and remaining grounded during turbulent times.

- Use Copal if you're looking for a deeper connection to yourself, the Hoodoo source, or the universe. This is the incense used for transcending or deepening the spiritual connections you already have.

- If you're looking for a tremendous all-rounded incense that attracts a bit of everything, you'll need some Cinquefoil. While not powerful, this is a fantastic pick-me-up incense or to help you stay motivated if you're already in a positive place.

The intensity and impact of incense spells can vary dramatically. Sometimes it can feel subtle, while other times, the effect can feel life-changing. It really depends on the experience, the incense, and where you are in your headspace.

However, if you're looking for something a little more powerful, consistent, and more dedicated, then you're going to want to use a spell. Shared below are some relatively beginner-friendly casts.

The Luck Draw Mojo

The Luck Draw Mojo spell is used to attract money into your life, be it through increased luck or good fortune. For example, if you're quoting a job to a new client and you want to aim high, or you're asking your boss for a pay rise, this is the kind of spell that will help you successfully secure the finances you're looking for.

Ingredients

- A red flannel pouch

- Magnetic sand

- A clove of garlic

- A lodestone

- Some sugar

- Some whiskey

Place both the lodestone and the garlic into the flannel pouch, pour in a shot of whiskey. Close it up and sprinkle some magnetic sand and sugar onto the pouch itself. Sew the pouch shut. As you go through this process, ensure you're speaking your intentions aloud.

The Serenity Spell

Life can feel turbulent, even at the best of times. This is why for many of us, it is important to take some time to find our peace, to return to a grounded state of mind, and just generally look after your health and wellbeing. Taking the time to perform a serenity spell is perfect for this, and it's relatively simple.

Ingredients

- 12 white candles

Wait until a full moon night and light all 12 candles in a circle around you. Sit comfortably for as long or as little as you like. While sitting, focus on your breathing and being present and grounded at the moment. Let the stress, anxieties, and worries fade away into nothingness as the moonlight, and the universal energy cleanses you and your being.

A Spell for Protection

No Hoodoo magic book would be complete without a protection spell. It's one of the most powerful and most universally applicable spells. Whether you're heading into a tough conversation, an emotionally draining situation, a hard time, or you're just looking out for yourself and your headspace, a protection spell can work wonders.

Fortunately, it's one of the simplest spells to perform. You need no ingredients or components. Just you and the words. Just say this spell to yourself, in your head or out loud, whenever you need it:

Pater noster dei sanctorum. Maria bella angelorum. Beautiful Mary sleeping. And the baby Jesus appeared to her in a dream. Dear, I dreamt that at the ordeal they brought you. Golden crowns lifted you up, and thorns have planted you. What you are saying is truth, the Christ answered to your mother. And whoever says this three times in a field is not afraid. Water, Thunder, and Lightning.

Just repeat whenever you need access to the protection. As you can tell from the cursive of the spells, this is a spell to help you not be afraid, no matter what you're facing, and that you're protected by the beings and spirits that are greater than you as an individual.

A Spell for Passion

Don't confuse this with a love spell. A passion spell is a way of increasing the connection and passion in an already-existing relationship, ideally between you and your romantic lover.

Ingredients

- Lavender Oil (3 Drops)

- Hot Sauce (3 Drops)

- Orris root pieces

- Whole peppercorns

- Three cups of rainwater

This spell is very easy to perform. What's more, you can essentially scale it up as much as you like. You can make as much or as little as you like, as long as you're using the ratios listed in the ingredients.

Take your ingredients and pour everything into a bowl and stir. While stirring, draw your attention to the heat of the hot sauce (the hotter the sauce, the more intense the spell will be), and focus on the temperatures and textures. If there are any smells, then this is what you'll want to focus on.

After everything has been stirred together well, take some of the mixture and sprinkle it at the front door to your house, or an entrance to a room or apartment. Cover this area well, and be sure to add some to the walkway. Now the lovers passing over this entrance will be driven by the increase in passion suggested to them by the supernatural forces you've invited to work alongside you.

With that, we draw to the end of this fine chapter. At this point, you have started a beautiful collection of spells that you can dip into and use to connect to the Hoodoo source whenever you need to. As for now, these spells should allow you to connect with your intentions (as well as helping to define them) with clarity, helping you in any situation or experience that you find yourself in.

Now it's time to move on to something a little more powerful.

CHAPTER FIVE

Rootwork Potions

"All hold that the Bible is the great conjure book in the world."

The final step in your introduction to Hoodoo magic still resides within the magical sphere of the practice, but this time focuses on the power of potions and other spells. These spells tend to lean more into the practice of rootwork and what you can expect from such a practice. Choose the ones you like as a starting point, but don't be afraid to try something new and branch out.

These are all potions and rootwork recipes passed down since Hoodoo was first established, but they serve as an entry point. There are certainly simpler and more complex recipes out there, so embrace the knowledge and dive in.

A Potion for Happiness

If you're looking for a way to boost your mood, to help you think more positively, and to help you focus on more productive outcomes, this is a potion that could benefit you greatly.

Ingredients

- A small potion pot, ideally with a cap or lid

- A dried and crushed dandelion

- One tablespoon of oregano (powder form)

- One tablespoon of cinnamon (powder form)

- One tablespoon of thyme powder

- Seven pine needles

Add all the ingredients into the potion pot, vial, container, or ampoule, and close it. Then, kneel facing East and hold the container in your hands to perform the spell, reciting Psalm no.7 seven times. It reads:

O LORD my God, I take refuge in you; save and deliver me from all who pursue me,

or they will tear me like a lion and rip me to pieces with no one to rescue me.

O LORD my God, if I have done this and there is guilt on my hands--

if I have done evil to him who is at peace with me or without cause have robbed my foe--

then let my enemy pursue and overtake me; let him trample my life to the ground and make me sleep in the dust. Selah

Arise, O LORD, in your anger; rise up against the rage of my enemies. Awake, my God; decree justice.

Let the assembled peoples gather around you. Rule over them from on high;

let the LORD judge the peoples. Judge me, O LORD, according to my righteousness, according to my integrity, O Most High.

O righteous God, who searches minds and hearts, bring to an end the violence of the wicked and make the righteous secure.

My shield[j] is God Most High, who saves the upright in heart.

God is a righteous judge, a God who expresses his wrath every day.

If he does not relent, he will sharpen his sword; he will bend and string his bow.

He has prepared his deadly weapons; he makes ready his flaming arrows.

He who is pregnant with evil and conceives trouble gives birth to disillusionment.

He who digs a hole and scoops it out falls into the pit he has made.

The trouble he causes recoils on himself; his violence comes down on his own head.

I will give thanks to the LORD because of his righteousness and will sing praise to the name of the LORD Most High.

This spell does take a little bit of time to cast and clearly comes from Christian origins, but after you've created the potion, you've got it indefinitely. Just take the vial around with you wherever you go, and it will bring you good luck while attracting happiness.

A Protection Spell for Your Home

If you are experiencing turbulent times at home, stressful or emotionally distressing situations, or the peace and wellbeing of your home are otherwise in jeopardy, then you can significantly benefit from this spell.

Ingredients

- A glass jar with an airtight lid

- Some broken glass

- Nail clippings from yourself or an animal (such as your pet)

- Some plugs

- Some glass wool

- A thistle

- Some Absinthe

Also, collect these components that you won't place in the jar:

- A pentacle of banishment or red felt to make one

- A consecrated black candle

- Banishing oil

Put all the ingredients listed above inside the glass jar and seal it. Place a pentacle of banishment on the lid. You can make a pentacle by cutting one out of red felt or using one you already have. Place the black candle dressed with banishing oil on the lid on top of the pentacle and light said candle. Now recite the following incantation:

Black candle and old curses, release your powers, reverse the flow of spells cast, leave pain and sorrow in the past.

Let the candle completely burn out. When it has, take the jar and bury it somewhere near your home, as close as you can get. If performed correctly and with intention, you will experience a protective shield around your home that should last up to six months. When the spell's power starts to diminish, simply repeat the process with a new jar.

A Potion for Prosperity

This is a powerful potion spell if you're seeking ways to boost success in any area of your life, whether in your career, personal missions, relationships, health, and wellbeing, or any other area of your life that you want to focus on.

Peace and prosperity are welcome and necessary in everybody's life, certainly at some point or another, and with this potion, you're sure to attract the right intentions that can help lead you to it.

Ingredients

- A jar (conventional glass jar will do)

- Three green and three gold candles

- Rosemary, bay, basil, thyme, lavender, and clove leaves (seven of each)

- Oil

- Three silver coins (any currency)

- A stick (wooden)

The recipe for this potion is relatively simple. Add all the herb leaves together into the jar, along with the coins, and cover everything in the oil. Then create a circle around the jar with the candles, alternating the colors as you go. Now light them.

Using the stick, mix the contents of the jar clockwise for seven rotations while reciting the magic words. Repeat this sequence of phrases seven times.

Paisa. Panam. Pecuina. Penz. Para. Dirua.

Now mix the jar contents in the opposite direction and repeat the next sequence of phrases seven times.

Aurid. Arap. Znep. Manap. Asia.

Now break the stick you were using to mix in half and put it in the jar, and leave the mixture in the circle, letting the candles burn out. Once they are gone, leave the jar somewhere in your house for it to bring prosperity into your home.

A Potion for Relationships (For Love and Friendship)

Your relationships are one of the most impactful areas of your life. In most aspects of this human existence, it's not what you know that will determine where you go and where life takes you, but who you know. It's the presence of others that will either raise you up to new heights or will hold you back profoundly. That's why it can be so special to develop a potion to help you attract love and friendship from the right people.

Ingredients

- Rosewater

- Three strawberries

- Three vanilla pods

- Three tablespoons of cocoa

- Three tablespoons of salt

- A saucepan

- A bottle (usually glass)

- A single sheet of people

- A red marker pen

Put your saucepan on your hob and place all your ingredients (minus your pen, paper, and bottle) into the pan, boiling for 30 minutes on a low heat setting. Now take your paper and, using your red marker, write the words:

"Pure love. Strong love. Open all the doors to me. Pure love. Strong friendship. Luck be favorable to me."

Roll up the paper when you're done and put it in the glass bottle before filtering the saucepan contents and pouring the now-soaked rose water liquid into the bottle as well. Close the bottle to ensure none of the content escapes.

From here, hold the bottle in your hands, shake it back and forth, and repeat the phrase that you wrote down seven times over.

A Potion for Making Someone Fall in Love with You

This may sound a little strange, but this is an effective spell that can be used in various situations for different reasons. The first that comes to mind is wanting someone to fall in love with you and want to be with you. While this is entirely possible with this spell (although I would recommend using the spell with care and caution), there are other uses you can consider.

For example, if your partner is stuck in an old way of thinking, is stressed, or isn't listening to you properly, they lack the compassion and empathy to keep the relationship balanced. This is a spell that can help remind them. If you seek forgiveness, this spell can help nudge their intention in this direction.

Ingredients

- A bottle of salt

- A few strands (a lock) of hair from the person you want the spell to resonate with

- Nine red, green, and yellow candles (nine of each)

Use the salt to create a circle of salt large enough for you to sit comfortably in and place the candles around the circle's edge, alternating the color with every candle, going from green to yellow to red, and so on.

Now sit in the circle and take your time lighting the candles one at a time, starting with the candle sitting in the most Eastern direction. In your right hand, hold the lock of hair and close your eyes. Say their name 99 times, making sure you picture the person as clearly as you possibly can in your mind's eye.

Let the candles burn out, and keep the same lock of hair in your pillowcase where you sleep for as long as you like.

Ishtar's Love Connection

Another spell you can cast to connect and form bonds of love with people in your life is by using Ishtar's Love Ligament spell. Ishtar is an ancient goddess in Mesopotamian religions, known as the goddess of war and sexual love. To cast a spell in her name is to draw on this ancient power to bring about love in your own life, to invoke love, compassion, and peace in others.

If you're looking for love in any area of your life, then this is a powerful, long-lasting spell that can create such an impact.

Ingredients

- A one-meter-long piece of red silk ribbon

Every night, for 48 nights in a row, tie a single knot in your silk ribbon while reciting the following incantation;

In the name of Ishtar, the one who makes everything fruitful, I tie you to me, and your love for me day by day as ivy on the wall will grow. So be it. So it will be.

On day 49, at dawn, as the sun starts to break the horizon, travel to a crossroads in a rural area or a place that you know to be connected with Hoodoo ancestry, and burn the ribbon, scattering the ashes into the wind.

The Powerful Negra Cinta

Personally, I don't condone using powerful Black magic spells on others. However, circumstances differ from person to person, and you may have reasons for performing such a spell. I am not here to judge, but I highly recommend that you move forward with extreme caution. I included this spell specifically for educational reasons but will not share others for safety reasons.

The Negra Cinta is a powerful Black magic Hoodoo spell that's designed for revenge. At the advent of Hoodoo magic, Black people would perform this on those causing significant harm, such as a slave owner or traders. It's a spell that redirects pain, trauma and suffering back at those who perpetrate it. However, it's an incredibly difficult spell to pull off due to how powerful its effects can be.

Ingredients

- A black candle

- A sheet of rolling cigarette paper

- Scorpion oil (alacran oil)

- Snake fat

- A black pin and black ink

- A parrot feather

- A black ribbon or black belt

- Black salt

- Cemetery land or a place connected with Hoodoo origins

You must ensure you're following the steps of this spell to the letter to ensure it's performed correctly. Start by engraving the name of the person you're placing the spell on onto the candle, using a knife of some kind. Pour the scorpion oil onto the engraving and sprinkle some black salt on it.

Let the candle sit for several hours upright before lighting it. Place a map of the person's geographical location of the person you're placing the spell on next to the candle, and write down the wishes, requests, curses, or actions you want taken against this person. Be sure to write them with the parrot feather and the black ink.

This is the part of the spell you want to perform carefully, making sure you're writing down what you want. You may want to show them the error of their ways, make them realize how horrible or nasty they have been, for them to experience how much pain they have caused, or whatever you want. Just write it on the map.

Now, cover the map with the snake fat and leave the set up alone until the candle has been burned completely. After that, fold up the map and hold it closed with the black ribbon, making sure to tie the ribbon in a knot seven times. Close the final knot with the black pin. As you tie each and every knot, you need to recite the following passage (totaling seven repetitions):

Forces of evil that since the times of times you rule the destinies of men, I invoke you to subdue with all your immense strength, every thought, word, and work of NN, that all go wrong to him, that no one listens to his cry and that all the evil that has caused me to return back to him/her and his/her family multiplied by 100. And so be it.

Once the candle has burned out, collect the remains alongside with your map, wrap everything together with the ribbon and the pin that should hold all the components together. Now bury everything far away from anything else on cemetery land. The spell will then start to take effect as the magic begins to flow.

There's a vast range of resources and information on other spells you can perform and what kind of incantations are possible, and it's all waiting for you to explore. For now, you have a solid platform to get started and experiment with what Hoodoo magic is capable of.

Now move forward, get started on this journey, and discover what the magic of Hoodoo can do for you.

Conclusion

The entire idea behind Hoodoo magic is to help you channel the power that already exists inside you in a productive way that benefits you, connecting you to the rest of the universe and the universal powers that be. Remember, this is magic that can be used in all areas of your life, whether you're trying to improve your luck, find prosperity, peace, better relationships, or clarity.

In essence, the core of Hoodoo is to improve your everyday life through intentions. This is achieved by accessing and connecting with yourself and your inner power and the power of our ancestors and our history. It's an incredible thing, and even if you're dubious, it's one of those practices that will get better in time, and the more you practice and open your mind to what's possible, the more you'll start to see the effects in your day-to-day life.

This book serves as an introduction to get you started, but the world of Hoodoo magic goes far deeper than what we've discussed. Once you've become familiar with the basics outlined in this book, you can continue with your explorations.

This means reading more books, specifically spell books, to further understand what you're able to achieve. It also means diving into your own exploration of the practice. Whether it is writing about your experiences, meditating, or tuning in to your own feelings and instincts, there's a lot you can discover by looking within yourself. If you have an instinctual drive to create a potion or to cast a spell that suits you, and you can feel the core of Hoodoo magic burning within you and nudging you in the direction of clarity, then more often than not, you're going to want to follow this lead.

Learn to trust yourself and your instincts. They can show you the world.

Remember, intentional thinking and practicing hoodoo magic can be a compelling and impactful journey. It can change your life, so make sure you're treating the knowledge, your own journey, and the experiences of others with respect and care. It would be foolish to underestimate what you can learn by traveling down this path.

For now, that's all from me. I hope you enjoyed this book and you learned something from it, and in some way, found some benefit in the text. If you did, then I would appreciate hearing back from you. You can do this by leaving a review on the site where you purchased your copy. For me, any feedback means the world and helps me to become the best version of myself, so I look forward to reading everything you have to say.

From here, I wish you all the best in the future, especially with your spiritual and magical endeavors. Good luck, and keep your mind open to learning and all the new possibilities that come with it. Until next time!

Thank you

Before you go, I just wanted to say thank you for purchasing my book.

There are many books on the same topic, but you took a chance and chose this one.

So, thank you for choosing me and for reading this book all the way to the end.

Now, I wanted to ask you for a small favor. **Could you please consider posting a review for the book? Reviews are the easiest way to support an independent author like me.**

Your feedback will help me continue to create books that will help you achieve the results you want. So, if you enjoyed it, please let me know.

www.ingramcontent.com/pod-product-compliance
Lightning Source LLC
Chambersburg PA
CBHW071217120626
46546CB00006B/2602